CW00701354

clan

bangarra
dance
theatre

stephen page + greg barrett

ALLEN&UNWIN

2014 marks Bangarra Dance Theatre's twenty-fifth year. Having reached this milestone I wanted to honour those people who have inspired Bangarra over the years by capturing our dancers in this extraordinary collection of images.

Dancers communicate so profoundly with the mere flex of a foot or hand, a shift of focus, the roll of a head, the transfer of weight within their body. As the dancers move in and out of space and light there is a momentum and energy, even with the smallest of steps.

Greg Barrett has so beautifully and skilfully recorded the dancers' magical, ephemeral moments in these intimate and dramatic photographs. Through Greg's vision for the company the images in this book capture the personal, the professional and the sacred moments of artistic expression.

These portraits are dedicated to the Aboriginal and Torres Strait Islander communities with whom we have built relationships, as our gift to them for the privilege of experiencing their traditional cultures and customs.

By having our feet in both worlds, of ancient and modern, Bangarra creates contemporary theatrical experiences that are influenced by timeless stories and customs. The land shapes the people, the people shape the language, the language shapes the song, the song shapes the dance, and the spirit flows through it all.

We are dedicated to spending time 'on country' in regional and remote communities, so our artists can refuel their spirits, and strengthen their sense of who they are and where they come from. They open themselves up to a process of discovery, connecting and re-connecting to the stories of their families and clans, to languages maintained and recovered, and to new ways of expressing their songs and dances.

Bangarra has been home to over one hundred talented artists from a myriad of Australian Aboriginal and Torres Strait Islander clans across this vast country. They come with their passion and raw energy, to embark on our physical and spiritual journey. Our dancers translate the ideas and visions of the choreographers, composers and designers into their special form of movement and artistry. They are the heart and soul of our clan.

I pay tribute to Bangarra's founding members, and to my Aboriginal families, the Nunukul and the Munaldjali clans of my parents and the Munyarryun, Yunupingu and Marika families of North East Arnhem Land. With their influence, guidance and spirit Bangarra has become its own clan.

I hope this photographic collection allows you to enter the world of Bangarra to experience the energy source of our work, to connect with our artists on a spiritual journey where every element is symbolic and infused with meaning.

stephen page
artistic director
bangarra dance theatre

I know little more today about Stephen Page than I did when I shared a bench with him and his brother, Russell, in a corridor outside a studio at Sydney Dance Company in 1993. We were there to make photographs for a book of contemporary dancers, *Danceshots*.

It was unsettling to be in their company: they both seemed reluctant to look at me as we spoke. Was it because they didn't want to be there, with this white man who was talking too much and so nervously? Or had I done something that I was unaware of to offend them? Or was it that the guilt I carried around in me was visible to Aboriginal people?

Despite my preoccupation with my awkwardness, and my own ignorance of how it was impolite to look too long into a stranger's eyes, it was clear that there was something extraordinary about them both.

Russell in his wonderful physicality: having just sat down he seemed ready to spring to his feet again. He could possibly be in two places, simultaneously.

Stephen seemed much more grounded, as if carrying an inner weight of darkness. Perhaps that was where he was looking, instead of at me; and when this was over he might go back to that darkness and begin turning it into dance.

I remember little about making the photographs, other than the discipline these men applied to the process. They had not fallen accidentally into having such superb technique. Even though they had been through formal, Western-based dance training, they were completely secure in their Aboriginality.

We made the photographs, shook hands, they left and I went on to take the next photograph with the next dancer. Then, soon after, I had a call asking if I would like to make some photographs for their newly formed dance company, Bangarra Dance Theatre.

And Stephen and I have been collaborators on an almost continuous basis since then.

To compare the experience of making this book with making a journey seems too facile, and yet it's very much like that: you come to it with your backpack of skills and knick-knacks and trepidation and anticipation and, even with the best research and with the collaboration of the superb dancers you see here, end up with a completely different experience to the one the guide books promised you.

Some time back the realisation came to me that, rather than fussing about my own feelings of guilt or inadequacies, or whiteness, or whether someone was or wasn't looking me in the eyes, the best way to proceed is to find a point of focus somewhere there in the middle distance and simply begin the journey and get busy with the making.

Twenty years after meeting Stephen, and Bangarra, this book is the result of that making, and a new setting out together.

greg barrett
photographer

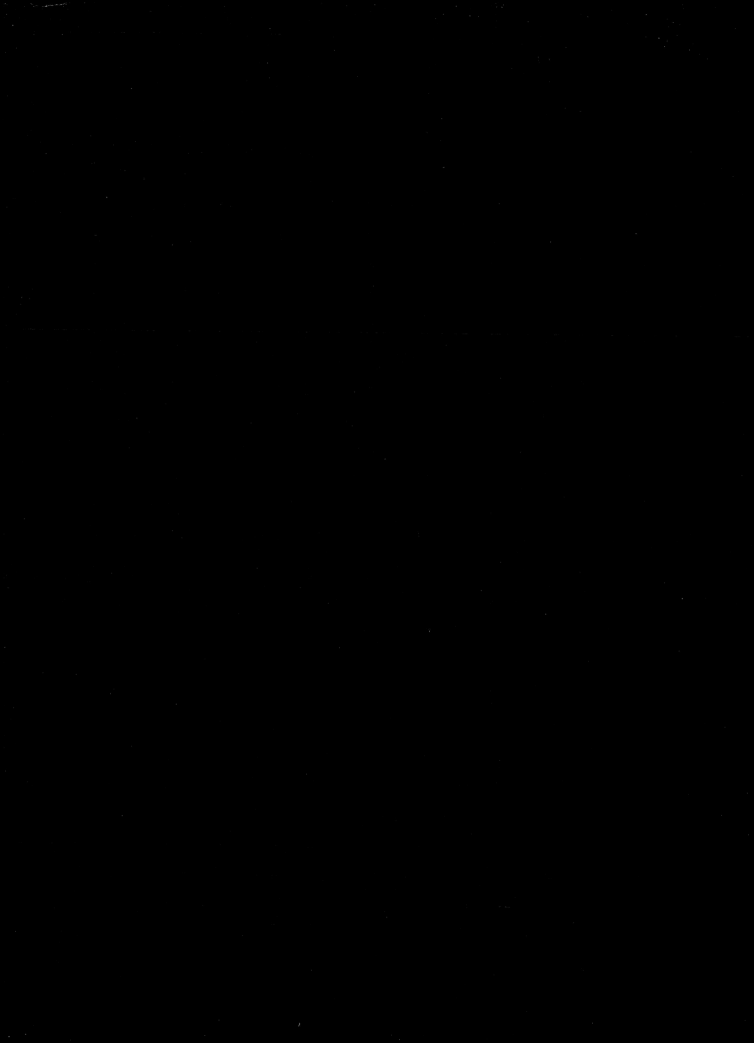

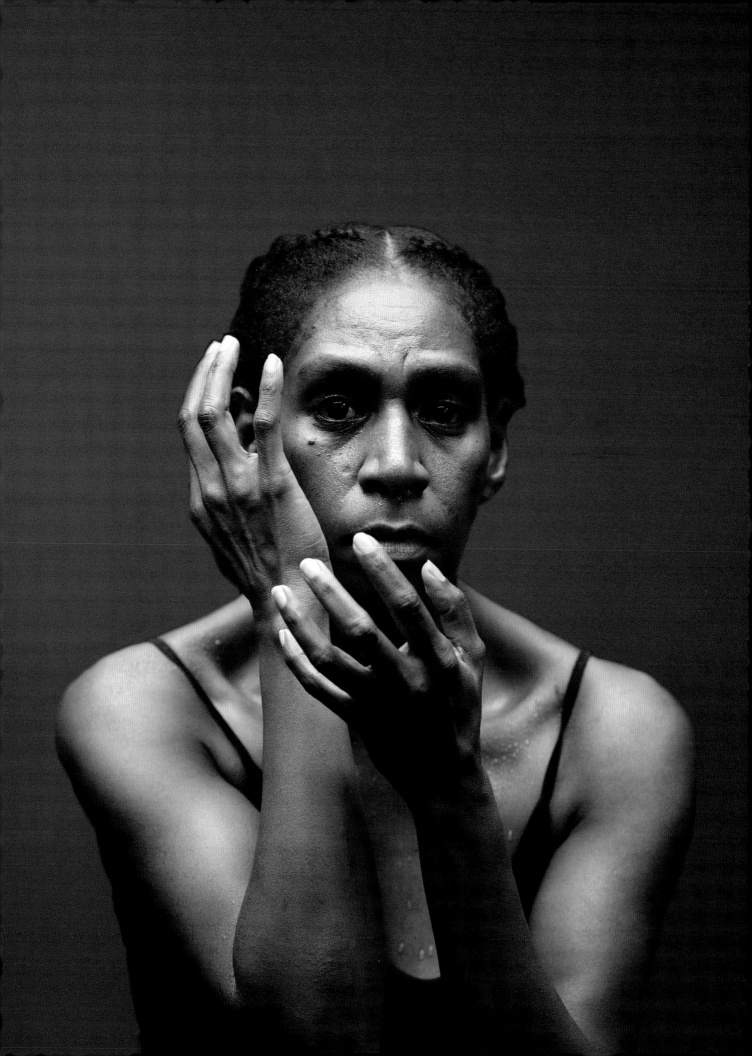

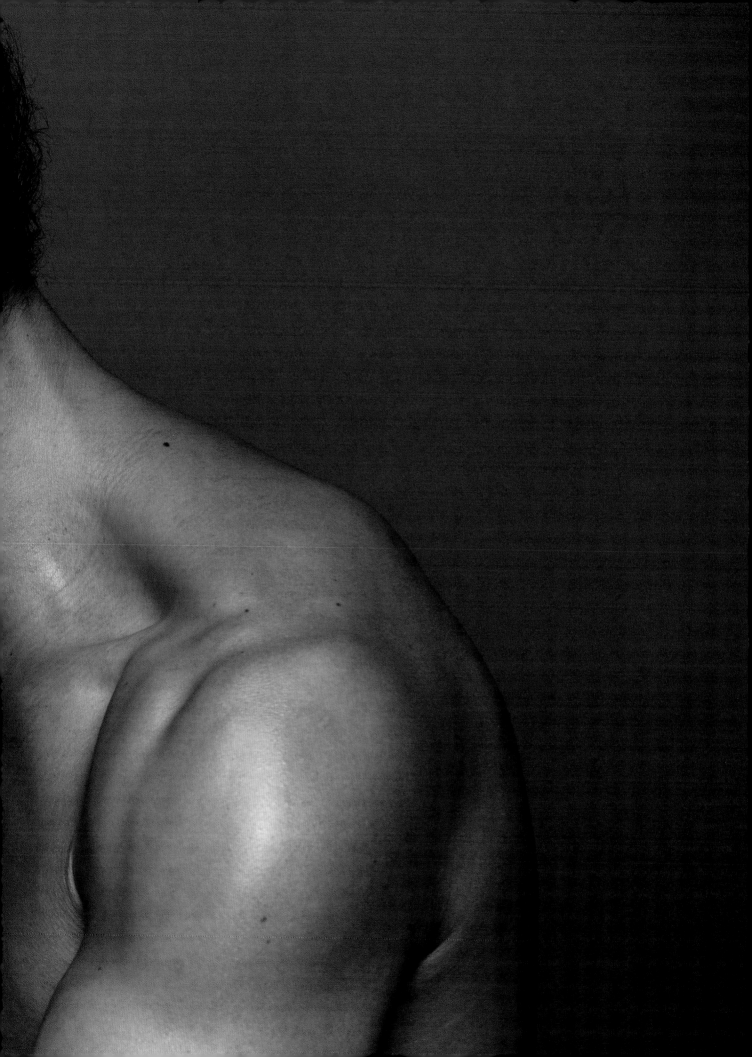

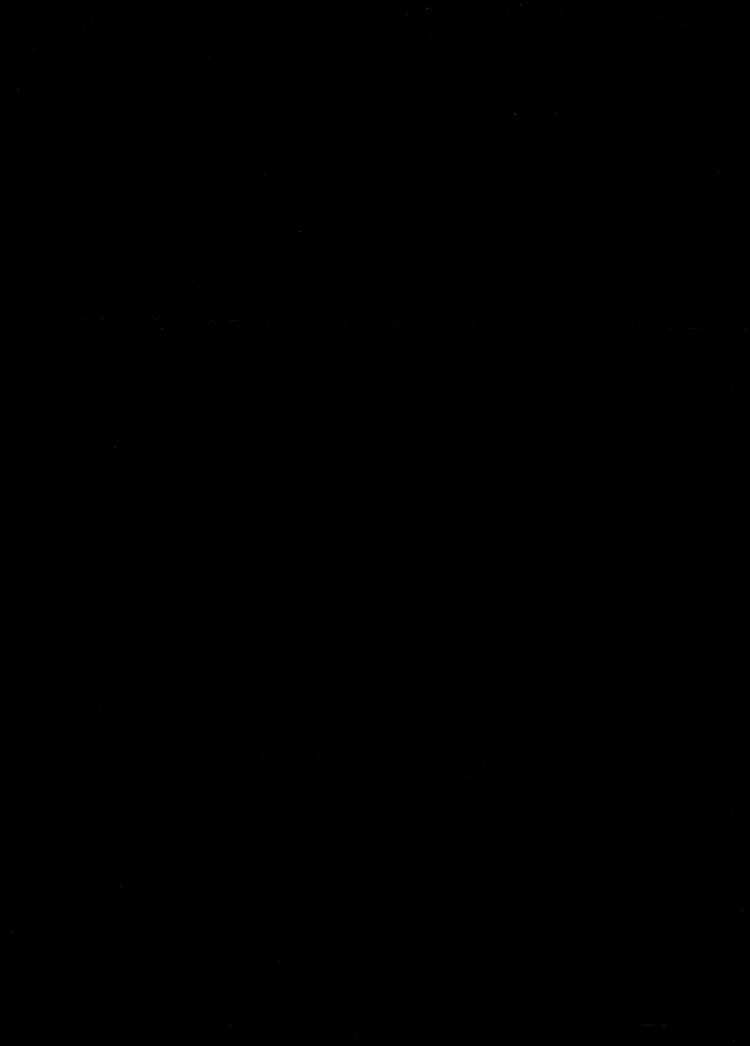

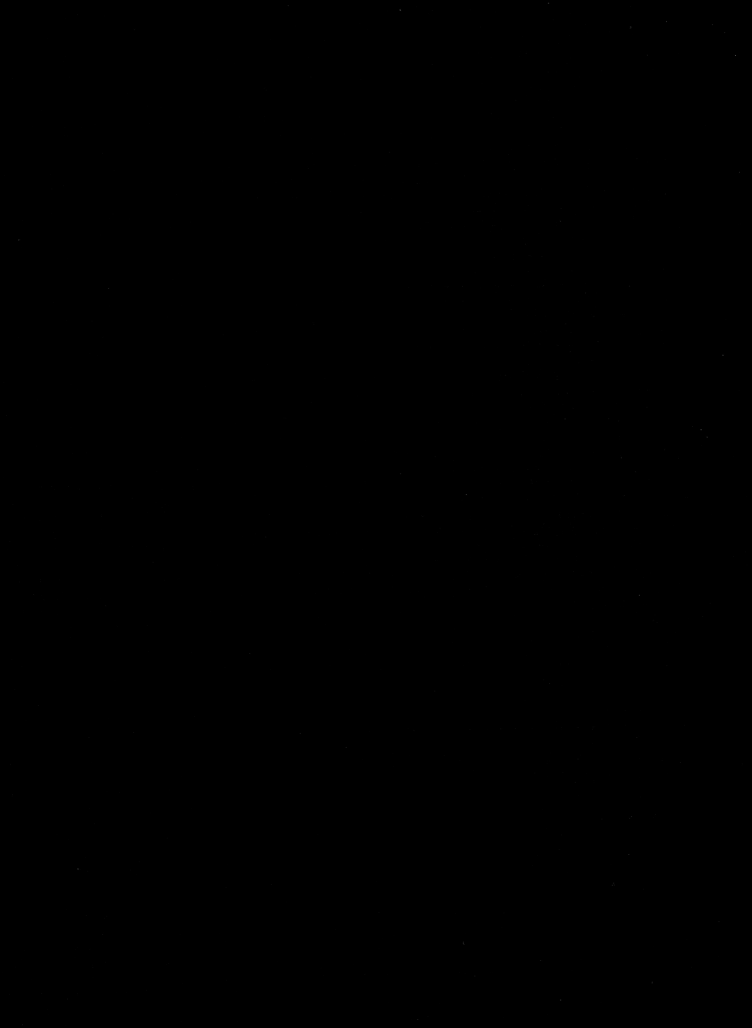

Kathy Balngayngu Marika

Born at Yirrkala in the Northern Territory, Kathy is a senior woman of her clan, Rirratjingu, the first clan and language group in that area.

Tara Robertson

Tara was born and raised in Darwin and is a descendant of the Munaldjali people from the Logan River area of Queensland.

Ella Havelka

Ella is a descendant of the Wiradjuri people in Western New South Wales.

Tara Gower

Tara is a Yawuru girl from Broome with Aboriginal, Filipino, Irish and Spanish ancestry.

Jasmin Sheppard

Jasmin is an Aboriginal woman with a mixed heritage of Irish, Chinese, Jewish and Russian ancestry. Her Aboriginal heritage is the Tagalaka and Kurtijar peoples, from Normanton and Croydon in the Savannah region, Gulf of Carpentaria.

Deborah Brown

Deborah is a descendant of the Wakaid Clan, Badu Island, and the Meriam people of Murray Island. Deborah also celebrates her Scottish heritage.

Elma Kris

Elma was raised on Thursday Island in the Torres Strait. She is a descendant of the Wagadagam, Kaurareg and Kai Dangal Buai peoples of the Western and Central Islands of the Torres Strait.

Yolande Brown

Yolande is a descendant of the Bidjara Clan of the Kunja Nation, Central Queensland, and also has French and Celtic ancestry.

Daniel Riley McKinley

Daniel's bloodline runs through the Riley Clan of the Wiradjuri people, from the Wellington area of Western New South Wales.

Jhuny-Boy Borja

Jhuny-Boy was born in Manila, The Philippines, and was brought up in the Outback town of Katherine in the Northern Territory.

Waangenga Blanco

Waangenga is a descendant of the Mer Island people and of the Pajinka Wik, Cape York.

Luke Currie-Richardson

Luke is a descendant of the Kuku Yalanji and Djabugay peoples, the Munaldjali Clan of South East Queensland and the Meriam people of the Eastern Torres Strait.

Leonard Mickelo

Leonard's family is from Cherbourg but he was born in Ipswich, Queensland. He is a descendant of the Wakka Wakka Tribe, Bidjara Nation, and the Kulilli Tribe, the Gungalhu Tribe and the Juduwa Tribe from Central Queensland. His other bloodlines are Chinese, Malaysian, Mongolian and Irish.

Kaine Sultan-Babij

Kaine was born and raised in Whyalla, South Australia. Of Aboriginal, Afghan and Croatian descent, Kaine's cultural and spiritual connections are to the Arrernte people of the Central Desert region in the Northern Territory.

A heartfelt thank you to:

My friend and collaborator Greg Barrett.

All the dancers of Bangarra, past and present. Your contribution to
our clan is invaluable; you are the spiritual instruments of Bangarra's
stories and performances, the flesh and blood of the company.
Thank you also for the inspiration you give to the next generation
of Indigenous artists and caretakers of our cultures.

All the choreographers, rehearsal directors, designers, story-tellers
and artists who have contributed to the celebration and continuation
of Aboriginal and Torres Strait Islander cultures through Bangarra
over the last 25 years.

The board, the production and management teams of Bangarra.

Stephen Page

Thank you:

Stephen and the Page family, for the opportunity to be part
of the making of this book.

The Bangarra family, past and present.

The dancers presented here for the skills, energy, knowledge,
patience and time they give, and gave, so generously.

Three remarkable women—Sue Hines, Catherine Baldwin and
Nathalie Vallejo, whose foresight, tenacity and faith in what we
might bring out of the seeming chaos of the studio, made
this book possible.

 Katie, Harpo and Osha, my other family and Home.

Greg Barrett

Bangarra Dance Theatre would like to pay respect to
and acknowledge the traditional custodians of the land
on which we gather.

First published in 2013

bangarra
DANCE THEATRE

bangarra.com.au

Bangarra Dance Theatre is assisted by the Australian Government through
the Australia Council, its arts funding and advisory body; and by the
NSW Government through Arts NSW.

Allen & Unwin

83 Alexander Street
Crows Nest NSW 2065
Australia

Phone: (61 2) 8425 0100
Email: info@allenandunwin.com
Web: www.allenandunwin.com

Cataloguing-in-Publication details are available
from the National Library of Australia
www.trove.nla.gov.au

ISBN 978 1 74331 413 5

Design by Lisa White
Printed and bound in China by 1010 Printing Limited

10 9 8 7 6 5 4 3 2 1